The Saltwater Diaries

First published 2020 by The Hedgehog Poetry Press

Published in the UK by
The Hedgehog Poetry Press
5, Coppack House
Churchill Avenue
Clevedon
BS21 6QW

www.hedgehogpress.co.uk

ISBN: 978-1-9160908-3-5

A CIP Catalogue record for this book is available from the British Library.

The Saltwater Diaries

Sue Burge

Contents

for Chris – who taught me to swim

Black Shuck

It begins with the call
        of flint on stone
the sand ablaze
        in the sinking light
a black dog, thin as shadow,
        sniffs the shoreline
salt contorts his muzzle
        into snarl and fang.

It begins with a storyteller,
        lean and lank,
scavenging the land
        for new words to spin,
the black dog, thin
        as seawashed bone,
and a woman lamenting her man,
        gone a year to the day.

It ends with clawmarks
        on a church door
a black dog, thin as the whip
        of the devil's tail,
eyes like Baltic amber, saltspun,
        ribs curved like the shattered
hulls he howls to the shore;
        a black dog
wearing his hunger like a shroud.

Black Shuck is the legendary hellhound who haunts the coast and countryside of East
Anglia. He is said to be the inspiration for the Hound of the Baskervilles.

Haibun - The Winter Sea

Stilled by the quietness of not-road, I take ruminative steps
on the frostfurred sand and discover a seal pup - spread-
eagled, a sack of self; clumps of whelk eggs, beached, each
papery cell a long, dry death. Cormorants play musical
chairs on the groyne posts; tip a gull from its perch. Fulmars
gossip of fish and thermals in their cliff nooks. A dog reads
the beach with his nose.

> low tide uncovers
> chalk reef - prehistory -
> bones sleep in the cliffs

A few months ago I swam here - is it the same water now?
We are all replenished over seven slow years, new cells,
fresh stomach linings. Will we know each other in the
spring, the sea and I?

> tide dragged
> cloud fallen
> sipped harvested swum

Foam frills the prom. Beach huts have been stormed askew.
The helter skelter coils its shiny silence. The pier is being
repaired. *Behind you,* it whispers, as I circuit the Pavilion
Theatre, home of THE ONLY FULL SEASON END OF
THE PIER VARIETY SHOW IN THE WORLD. The
pier remembers the slap of flip-flops, rhythmic as a
hangover. Barnacles feast on its underbelly. The town
hibernates. Only coffee and second-hand books on offer.

> do not blink
> witness the turn of the tide
> believe your eyes

Haar*

It rolls from the sea
like a forgotten myth
of demon's breath

covers us like brides,
a world silent as snowfall.
It will rise again

as all things do
leaving us with lashes
damp as grief.

How we flinch at the slow reveal
of horizon, field, lane
how easy it was

to inhabit that quiet
smudged landscape
like characters in Brigadoon
shoreless, blurred, unrequired.

*a cold sea fog

11

Where Ted and Rita Lived

Strips of tan tights bind rose stems to trellis,
they shrivel like dying balloons as we snip.

Floorboards fuzzed with scaly dust, the colour
of old salt; walls pollocked with tea-stains,
ketchup daubs, the scrape of sensible shoes.

Maybe once there were children, two,
swaddled in home-knitted crewnecks, one plain,
one purl, churring along to *The Clangers*
in the room where I sit and tweet *#soupdragon.*

We find a bright Gonk in a dark corner.
Sometimes our bedroom walls overhear stories:
Mr Pinkwhistle, Mrs Peppercorn, The Magic Faraway Tree
and we sway and smile in our lullabied sleep.

I think of them still as I sew curtains
to shade the view of the sea -
pin, tuck, hem, break the thread.

A Conversation with my Father

You wouldn't know these plants – seablight, orach, samphire turning to flame – but you'd be curious, eager to assimilate these edgelands. You're more familiar with river than saltmarsh, with the Thames - tamed to urban needs. You'd know the birds of course, a curlew's call boomeranging on the wind, knots rising in a skeltering plume; you'd recognise the halyard's tick, want to stitch the gape of weatherworn wrecks back together again. I can almost feel your hands on my ribs, lifting me, four years old again. *Look,* you'd say, *this boat is part of the land now, beyond our help.* And I'd wonder at the height of a tide that could bring a whole world inside this old husk.

You don't like silence, cramming it with bad jokes, maddening clichés; stories we've both heard before. *Listen,* I want to say, *to the space between us. It's okay to fill it with the silence of two people watching an egret place its foot in the slowest of slow motion.* You'd turn your good eye towards me, carry on along the path, blued with crushed mussel. I suppose the path is us, the occasional impasse, soft blur of stagnant water, curves and swerves of tidal detritus, something pushing, unseen, blistering the mud.

Headspin

There are days when herons teeter
high on thick-branched trees
their gaze hooking the fishless horizon
where once upon another time, I saw
a sassy woman on the towpath
in a dress shiny as an over-ripe cherry
singing a Bizet earworm I've never dislodged.

There are days when I convince myself
life's clear as a few brisk lines on an Etch A Sketch;
nights when I stir, dream-deep,
write down my innermost thoughts,
then, when I'm properly awake, read:
carrots, bones, elastic bands, phone Dad.

There are days when I feel like a giant girl
in a doll's house, pretending to be grown up,
a house built of bricks baked
from the stinking mud of the Thames,
bricks that still carry the wash of waves.

Today I push like Alice, my arm-span too wide,
forehead tipping up, up, flat against the ceiling,
hearing the muttering of tides,
the herons in their too-high nests,
Carmen tattooing the towpath
with a *faran faran farandella*
and me with my too-full head
pushing out, out, against the knit of my bones.

Holkham Hall

Before, the sea would come to where the door is now.
It took centuries to lure to a new and dune-strewn shore
trailing salt and wrack in its surly wake.
Now gulls wheel over furrows rimed with frost,
Egyptian geese babble in their pharaoh tongue
through bee-stung beaks, their scrabbling feet
stippling a tamed lake, serpentine only in name.
Once, the thatched icehouse was crammed with the dirty
freeze of Danish waters – a gin, a tonic, the clink
of cholera. The butler in his thrice-shone shoes treads,
surprised by the grind of sand, the crunch of salt,
the wisps of marram in the swirls of oxblood Axminster,
by the lull of waves in each neat tuck of the linen-press.

Nightcombing

The sea dozes, lulled by its own monotony. She pries shells from the hearts of hagstones, plenty of salty gristle at every tug and pluck. Out there, where the sea is taller than thirty men, red lights flash. A coven of boats gather at the cauldron's rim, under the sign of the inverted plough, Orion on his head, belt adrift. Both of these are correct. Her feet have walked for miles on the same tilting square of sand, watch-hands turning like a crazed compass. She's late, she's late for every important date. *Come walk through my clefty shadows*, says the cliff, in the voice of an aunt she never knew. The moonlight on her skin turns her face to mould.

Revenant

It's not long before this landscape reclaims me -
wind pistolwhips my city skin
    scours my nostrils clean of Paris's siren scent

and, already, I'm asking my urban alter-ego
    was it only yesterday I walked over Pont St Michel
    mourned the wounded limbs of Notre Dame
    joined in the shrug and pout of a different tongue?

now the sea's voice drowns the memory of buskers' chanson
    the squeal and hiss of stop-start metro in Paris's sour belly

        Paris, who ate herself hollow then spewed out
        boulevards in elegant limestone

    as the sea chews cliffs into overhang
    reveals hearth, weapon, bone

gorsepricked, I dream for a hundred years, how once
    I lay listening to the snug hum of puffins in burrows -
envied them their little metropolis, their certainty of *home*

and when I wake up it's lunchtime
    the wind hinders the air with wildsong;
    I am ready to listen.

Canal

The canal is full of winter
rooks spin in the air
like starlings
magpies
flank each bank
tuxedoed

lock gates
like quote marks
single   double
contain
the water's words
its wonderings

and maybe love
is like this too
a series of checks
and compromises
to keep things level
the surface calm

the mist holds the moor
to ransom
there are distant bleats
from barcoded sheep
packhorse bridges
beer bitter as rue

Lure

The windows have been weeping
for hours.   I head for the rainpocked

sand, watch a matinee of dogwalkers.
I want to write your name in stones

to draw a shaky heart around
something my tongue has lost.

The ebbing tide pulls at the salt
in my blood. The sea knows

I'm just a formula, H_2O
with a pinch of salt

that's learnt to walk. Today
I'm only half an equation.

Sometimes I wonder if it's you
calling me, your saltiness

leaving tidemarks on my skin.
Or is it the sea who wants me

to put on my tail, slice open
my fins, slide back in?

Marginalia

Today I am full of winter -
unnatural with mucus and itch,

blazing in the high sun's limelight.
I plough feverish, liminal lines

between sea and road, verges busy
with the denim strut of cornflower.

An unmoored pillbox strains on shingle.
I have a mood board of pebbles in my pockets.

Quadruple strands of ragged wire
close in on my wandering skin.

There are signs. The idea of keeping out
and keeping in. The land trembles

around a broken boat - rag and bone yard
of single flip-flops, paint flakes, a toothless saw.

I recall the low, twisted spread
of an oak maddened by decades of wind.
Someone asks me if I have seen glow-worms.

Ariel Rising

Epileptic, he says, darkening his prescription pad. *Like
your mad Aunt Juana,* mouths Mum to Dad. A fluke, my
just-crawling hand finding the sharpness of a shattered
lightbulb, spasming at the first sight of my own blood. The
sharpness enters me then, like a fragment from a
sorcerer's mirror. I am taboo, labelled, banned. A
barbiturate junkie before I can walk. My slothful blood,
saturated. Pocketing my tiny brown bottle of suicide, *Eat
me, Eat me.* But inside I'm a mayfly, struggling upwards
through this thick, brown litany of *can't * * * Misdiagnosis,*
declares a young doctor four decades later, unwriting my
life. Two twitching years to unknit the ravel in my blood
and then, like Ariel, I'm unbound, blood light and pure as
air.

Riptide

Vasovagal syncope   it sounds like
an artefact   a treasure from the deep
this rising in me   a neap tide racing
submerged for three times one hundred
seconds   ungilled   comatose
in my shroud of silt   then bloodsurge
jerks me like a fish in a keepnet
with one convulsive reboot   I emerge
a scaly Lazarus mouth unclogging
                I'm okay, I say
but resurrection renders me liminal   chthonic
sometimes   head down in mock dive
I stay afloat   pupils heroin-wide
breath caught like a fishbone
body scarred with salt lines
last time   this time   next time

Wild Swim

You swim like you're drowning;
I worry that you can't float.

I'm out deep. Level with my eyes,
the horizon is a bowl,

its dark rim magic-markered.
A swallow skims my periphery;

I can hear the sea thinking
in a calm yet rusty way.

I swim like a *Thunderbirds* puppet
in my wetsuit, making stiff sea angels

on my back. You're paddling,
toes tentative at the water's edge

worried that I swim too well,
that I am thalassic, suffixed by mer-
end-stopped by brine.

Talisman

Inspired by a Tlingit carving of a captive witch

Whalebone witch, you have crawled the length
of two oceans to nestle in my outstretched palm

here where sand, gravel and mud shapeshift the shore
where wave turns seals from land-blubber to sinew.

Your body is androgyne, serried with dirt-grained
sickles of rib or breast or stigmata.

When I hold you, I am not soft girl, unshelled,
I am Hippolyta, carapaced in sisterhood, roughened

by the draw of a bow. I am Daphne, newly crowned,
safe in my bark fortress. Whalebone witch

with your yellowing salt-scoured skin,
the mark of rope stark on your back-bound arms,

your saucer eyes upturned to uncertainty, mouth
wide with memories of whale-song and knife.

Salt Road

River, you and I carry our hidden cargoes lightly.
I am a container for 40 measures of salt,
an untold recipe, and you, River, you are brim
with dissolved salts, your easy flow just scientific
sleight of hand. Here we are, you and me, *agua dulce*,
marching towards the cocksure honesty of the sea.

I remember the Dead Sea cradling me like flotsam,
hair tangled into Gorgon spikes, sun peeling
my abraded skin. I remember how upright
became alien, how the siren call of 'float'
took me almost beyond saving
into feverish visions of past lives -

> *a Roman soldier, paid in salt to guard*
> *the Via Salaria, sweat drying on my skin*
> *in the shape of pale kingdoms;*
> *an Anglo-Saxon, panning the river*
> *for white-gold, fingers brine-burnt,*
> *rough as sackcloth.*

But I am here now, racing with you, River,
a diluting rain pouring from sagging skies. Mud
tugs at my boots, my footprints are crucibles,
gorse pulls at my clothes. I am unlaced, unpinned,
ready to sink, to feed you with my sluggish silt,
ready to rise and fall again.

And Winter Came Suddenly

A day of skies so batwing dark
the town turns on its night-time lights
and strings of starlings straggle back
with tales of hollow bellies, craving beaks.
The rain falls straight in backlit lines
and all around the town is calm
until cats awake and prowl and kill,
chained dogs howl and hedgehogs hide.

It's on a day like this, with seas
like mountains, cold and high,
that you walk those crumbling cliffs -
candy-striped in sandstone, carrstone, chalk,
face out towards the curve of the world,
despair etched through your core like seaside rock,
body ticking out its final pulse,
arms spread wide in a perfect dive.

The Unreliability of Clouds

There were no clouds where I grew up
for all good fairytales take place in the forest
between the shapeshifting shadows.

When I hear the word for the first time
it is too close to "clout" and "loud".
I ask my unborn brother what it means,
instantly forgetting his answer.

One day a low cloud catches on a dead tree,
light as a cotton boll, as a wig.
This is the day my mother begins to die,
it takes her a lifetime to do so.

Gradually, I get to know them better.
Now I sleepwalk in the encyclopedia of clouds
full of moonshadows and ravens
defecating in the blackness.

I used to dream of being a weathergirl,
envying their power to move clouds
over land and sea.

Sometimes clouds appear like speech-bubbles
broadcasting my untold thoughts.
I realise that each one is unique as a thumbprint,
though many are clichés.

Some are like sex, rumpled and knowing,
sashaying across the sky with sassy curves;
often, they shadow my white clothes in passing
with an unbleachable darkness.

At day's end the clouds look like bruises,
smell like vanilla.

Beached

A fat bee squeezes into a Schiaparelli-pink flower, pheasants wind themselves into the air like creaky cogs; the marram grass whispers. A container ship floats in the sky like a steampunk vessel. Below its bulk she can see the dark line of a false horizon, as if the wet thumb of the artist has smudged out the end of the world and started again. The beach is strewn with starfish, thousands - limbs puckered, vibrating with dehydration. She lies beside them. *What happened?* she asks in her starfish voice, but the answers are too faint to understand. She may be in a dream she's had before. The stars crackle overhead, streak the sky with their deaths. The artist arrives with a barrow, loads armfuls of starfish, strings them into a chandelier and hangs it in the church overlooking the saltmarsh. For days there are salt stains like teartracks on the cracked tiles in the nave. She sits and waits. *I will wake up soon,* she tells them, denying the taste of blood in her mouth.

The Saltwater Diaries [extract]

Some days I leave my other self
sealed in my aunt's liver-spotted mirror
and come here to explore the wreck's
dark ribs, where I meet a faceless man
searching for a shoreless land.
Once, he discovered a boat
full of ballast, added his weight;
sailed the warp and weft
of the known seas.

*

I had a floor the colour of damp sand,
when I walked across it
my toes puckered.

*

Storm warning – beach huts collapse
like movie props and beached on the sand
there's a whale who turned left
instead of right.

*

Miranda, storm-child, eyes full of spells.
Here she is, drawing Ferdinand's lovesick
mouth down to her saltiness,
twice breached,
as Prospero weeps, reads enchanted pages
rippling like kelp, and Caliban
folds himself into a mudhole
waiting for her lust to darken once more.

*

I sew you a letter in a pouch
cut from dead fishermen's trousers
dear ocean
my face pressed against the cold
slippage of the window
the shudder of distant thunder.

My letter box is full of junk mail
about Dramamine, Benadryl,
flood insurance.

*

I shimmy into my indigo ballgown,
play hide and seek with my tail.
My skin leaks.

I wake to the doormat's
wet spikes, salt stains raging
down the door panels.

It takes hours for the brine
to reach my eyes,
to fill my open mouth
with the world's salt.

Sea Glass

When I lick you, sea glass, you taste of pistachio,
crushed sage. On my palm, grainy as a sugared almond,
you weigh less than a fulmar's egg, more than a grey feather.

You could be three times older than me, or more,
but I like to think you are the echo of that glass
I smashed when the world was too bitter to swallow.

Sea glass, you hold the answers to unasked questions
in your salty heart. I want to cleave you, hang you
from my ears, catch the chink of your pasts as I turn my head.

Understory

I am surprised by the geometry of trees,
> how they encompass every degree and angle

how sometimes they are a sigh, sometimes lively as the sea
> the air all ripple and lap around them

how they observe our quick growth into angels and bullies,
> hold our tall and tangled tales in their languid sap.

Today I am lichen-crusher, footprinting the woods' pungent underbelly –
> there are fungi, fleshy, nippled like a sow.

A low branch cradles me -
> I am a nursery rhyme caught in a fairytale.

The trees are patient, waiting to set the world on fire, releasing
> a few pale forerunners before the dying year's *hurrah*.

A rook shouts, a lost chicken frets by the path on scaly legs,
> jungle fowl, more welcome, perhaps, than me.

They say you only have ten childhood memories

Fried eggs cooling, a pool of ketchup to dip
the pointed ends of the white bread in,
mum pushing a cloth under the door,
rivulets on the kitchen floor like dog wee
and it feels like the dark's seeping through
the wallpaper.

*

      I wish for a windowless room in a high tower
away from this tip-tap-tapping like the fingers
of all the world's bogeymen.
      I stick out my tongue, taste dust, metal, fox.
There's a conspiracy of raindrops.
I've forgotten what blue is like, I say
but mum's mumbling over her busy mop
and there's a stain on the ceiling in the shape
of Denmark.
      And it's rain, rain that makes me want
to believe in God again.
      Rain, rain like hard prayers on rosary beads.
I chant wishes like spells
      rain, rain go away.

*

In my bedroom there's a pink plastic umbrella
frilled like an anemone
and my patent shoes for best
but my feet are webbed like swan maidens.
      Rain, rain like white noise.
      Rain, rain until my mouth's a pock
between two gills
and all around me fish unfurl
like Christmas cracker fortune-tellers
      today you will be unlucky until 4pm.

All the water there will be, is

I paddle in the ford - an upright Ophelia
stinging nettles whisper of impossibilities
grasp grasp, they rasp
and the river agrees with its throaty yellow voice

I want to take a picture of how the river sounds
a sharp black line of rill and trickle
like the rise of a blackcap's song,
the white noise of its eddies

what if I drop this notebook in the water
see my words blur, nothing more than
the buzz buzz buzz
of my urban mind

a dog enters the ford, nose to the surface
as if the meniscus holds old smells
        the musk of dead deerhounds
        the slink of fox
        a footstep softened by rain

the water is alive
with invisible obstacles
submerged memories
my toes enfold the slick gemstone shine
        of stone

dragonflies - a dark flit - trace messages
over the water
        live your life in four directions
        upstream downstream cross-stream east
        and cross-stream west
their iridescent script dissolves in the air

I wade upstream, away from the cleave of goosegrass,
worry when I lose the seashell-to-the-ear tinnitus rush
of the river's voice
a drought, a dam, maybe sadness has sent it underground
I listen for the return of its fleshy suck

a sudden sign shouts: *Danger Deep Water* -
        I think I will be good at floating
        will like the feeling of my ears
        filling with wash and brink

        how the brisk quickstep of my heart will slow
        as I drift closer to the cling of lichen
        a shroud of duckweed parting in my wake

Contagion

He smells of mahogany
fingers tunnelled with old cuts
webbed with the clean dirt of work
oiled with the sap and pitch of pine.

The curve of a well-planed plank,
a nail the exact length to embed -
when he raises his head his eyes
are empty as a dredged river.

The men who sail his finished craft
become prone to melancholy.
They weep overboard, toy with their food,
daydream the heft of the right length of rope.

Window

She cannot stop looking at this new middle ground – the
allotments where a man appears daily, a man with skin the
colour of dug earth, clothes the colour of wilt; a man who
contemplates his plot with the severity of Descartes. He
does not look like the kind of man who would own a cat.
Perhaps she has imagined him.

There is, of course, a whole world off-frame, but she
prefers her vision to be held this way.

At the vanishing point the sea tilts, the cliffs loom. She
thinks about the mammoth found there. Did it die upright
in a Pompeiian rush of mud and tide? Then, the slow
millennial reveal, bone by patient bone.

Sometimes the judder of a passing car catches her
unawares, sometimes there's the manic ripple of a green
woodpecker's call, the thrust of a ship too close to land,
the urge to straighten the frame, step back, breathe. The
fear of losing all that is contained.

Pup

fly-silvered husk   once was pup   once was wide-eyed
   now waterlogged skinbone
                  now flipper-limp   tiny-nailed like toddler
nearby sister-pup   maggot-rippled   open-jawed in final bleat
   sister pup   nearby   greyfurred   flatdamp
sniffed by loll-tongued spaniel   hole-eyed boy-pup   girl-pup
              salted to the sand
   once was   pup   once was

I Believe in the Sea

If there is a god, I think he would look like Brian Blessed and live in the sea. I think he'd like that. He'd be closer to creation, by which I mean us. He could be quiet and deep now that heaven is full of warplanes, their dark wings folded, ready to dive.

I think he'd want to hold the drowned, tell them how it's not their fault, how they didn't understand the word "rip", how it lurks toad-like, just below the surface.

He would like how the alexanders on the sea-path bake in the sun, inky as the devil's tail. He would especially like the knit of colour on the saltmarsh. He could wear it as a vestment as he listens to the hymn of the wind through grass, the countering tenor of bittern, the soprano *ping* of bearded tit. He would appreciate the cormorants opening their wings in hallelujah.

Sometimes I gather him a ditty bag of beachcomb. Seaweed like bronchioles, a scallop shell's eroded tracery, a scoop of sea phlegm, a dogfish – skin shed, teeth bared for a forgotten meal, desiccated body forever swimming towards his patient wife. Maybe god has seen it all before, but I like to think he would examine my offerings, enjoy the madness of texture and grain, before composing a vast and powerful prayer.

What is it about trees that makes me want to cry

You once told me about an apple tree
your father planted on the day of your birth.
I want to find that tree, celebrate its regular deaths,
applaud how it shrugs leaves like a snake shedding skin,
its dormant sap.

Long ago, an elm fell behind me with a long, rasping
sigh of displacement, a sound that would have made
Archimedes shout "Eureka!"
The friend I was with said she was elsewhere,
but her fingerprints prove otherwise.

I love the certainty of twigs, the chemical green-ness
of new growth, the unassailability of roots,
the bitterness of bark. I love touching
the Judas Tree, how it haemorrhages purple blossom
like traitor's blood.

Your latest Instagram post is of snowfall
crushing the trees in a temple garden.
I imagine how they will feed on its thaw, heal.

I realise I love your apple tree best in winter
for the space in between it leaves for me,
how its monochrome outline cannot rustle
or whisper behind my back.

The tree I fear most has a message carved,
thigh-high to an adult, by a boy who died
before he learnt to write.

At night I wear my crown of thorns, dream
of chainsaws and axes, of muntjac sniffing
at trunkless trees. I want to ask the trees
if they are scared of the dark.

I imagine Anna and Vronsky meeting, fur-trimmed,
by a grove of silver birch, making frantic
frost-forged declarations.

This morning a nest fell at my feet
seven freckled eggs
one for every month you've been gone.

Trompe l'oeil

We collect pebbles burnished by the turning tide, our footprints reconfigured by the moondrugged water, grain by grain. When we take the path up to the trees, I think I can still see water through the leaves, but it's just dark air, and I remember that woman who sculpts space - the underneathness of chairs, the insideness of rooms. We emerge to an ironbright sky, punctured like a piñata by the rooks' calls into a steady rain that slicks the earth. There will never be more of us above the ground in this shifting airiness than the millennia of crowded dead below, so I tread carefully, wonder who is there with their cells sliding and merging in the dampness under my sandalled soles. Now we're back down the gulley to the beach again, sand roughened by drizzle and lugworm casts, and I look at you and you seem to be smiling.

Acknowledgements

Trompe l'oeil appeared in **Under The Radar**, a version of *The Saltwater Diaries* appeared in **The Interpreter's House** and *The Unreliability of Clouds* appeared in **Strix**. *Nightcombing* is included in the **Valley Press Anthology of Prose Poetry** and *Ariel Rising* is forthcoming in the Emma Press anthology on illness. *Marginalia* appeared in the November 2019 Aldeburgh special edition of **Coast to Coast to Coast.**

Thanks to the Norwich Stanza Group, led by Julia Webb, for all their feedback on many of these poems and to The Runton Wreckers, led by the inimitable Peter Pegnall, for their insights which helped to make many of these poems stronger. I am grateful to Jonathan Ward, Anne-Marie Fyfe and Rachel Piercey – many of these poems were written thanks to their inspirational workshops. Huge thanks to Heidi Williamson for her advice, insight and never-ending support. Massive thanks to Chris Cullen for his support, generosity and for always, ungrudgingly, helping to create the time and space for me to write. And last, but very much not least, to Mark Davidson at Hedgehog Press for having such faith in my work and Isabelle Kenyon for proofreading.